Scripture Out Loud!

Dramatic Readings for Lent and Easter
Marianne Houle and Jeffrey Phillips

Augsburg Fortress
Minneapolis

SCRIPTURE OUT LOUD!
Dramatic Readings for Lent and Easter

References used for introductions to the individual dramas include:
Bruggemann, Walter, et al. *Texts for Preaching: A Lectionary
　　　Commentary Based on the NRSV–Year B.* Louisville:
　　　Westminster John Knox Press, 1993.
New Interpreter's Bible. Vols. 1, 8, and 9. Nashville: Abingdon Press,
　　　1995.
The New Revised Standard Version Bible © 1989 Division of Christian
　　　Education of the National Council of the Churches of Christ in the
　　　United States of America.

Various translations of scripture were paraphrased to create the drama
scripts.

Cover Design: Barsuhn Design
Cover Art: Jane Pitz
Editors: Dennis Bushkofsky and Rebecca Lowe

Manufactured in the U.S.A.

ISBN 0-8066-3964-4　　　　　　　　　　　　　　　　　　　　　3-3964
03　02　01　00　99　　　　　　　　　　　　　1　2　3　4　5

CONTENTS

Welcome . . .

to *Scripture Out Loud!* The idea for a book of short, lectionary-based dramas arose from a real need at the Congregational United Church of Christ in Arlington Heights, Illinois. For several years, Marianne Houle, a fourth through sixth grade church schoolteacher, was unable to interest bright, attentive students in lectionary-based Bible readings. Even though the children enjoyed the lessons from the curriculum, when it came time to read the assigned scripture passage, they lost interest—and heart.

Marianne experimented with ways to make the scripture readings more accessible to children in her class, while remaining faithful to the biblical text. Dramatic renderings provided an answer. Indirect speech could be transformed into direct speech, difficult words could be simplified, and less central material could be omitted. Sometimes interpreting the biblical text required adding a character, rearranging the material, explaining context, or removing certain phrases. Simple props, costumes, stage directions, and lighting added interest. Most importantly, each child could have a role in the drama—a *personal* experience with the Bible passage. The goal was not to stage a Broadway production every Sunday morning, but to convey God's word so that it engaged the students and made sense to them. The dramas served to supplement the main goals of the church school curriculum.

The results of dramatic scripture readings in class were exhilarating. The impassive reading of scripture stories was transformed into dynamic enactment of them. The children became the characters, the stories took on life, and scripture came alive. Since they understood the readings, the students were motivated and prepared to delve into the rest of the curriculum and learn even more.

With the success of the dramas came the idea to share this discovery with other church schoolteachers and groups. Confirmation classes, youth groups, vacation church schools, summer camps, after-school programs, and even Sunday morning worshiping assemblies could use the dramas to convey scripture readings.

Concerned that the dramas be faithful to scripture and that they be grounded in an ecumenical and liturgical context, Marianne approached Interim Pastor Jeffrey Phillips, and asked for his assistance. Jeffrey was impressed with the concept and by the results he had seen in Marianne's church school class. He agreed to help, and *Scripture Out Loud! Dramatic Readings for Lent and Easter* was begun.

Spreading the good news to all ages

Marianne and Jeffrey selected twelve passages from the time between Ash Wednesday and the Day of Pentecost. Many churches are interested in using dramatic renderings of the Bible—especially during this time of the year. Indeed, Lent and Easter are dramatic and holy seasons.

In its own way, Scripture Out Loud! is part of several new developments in churches across the country. The first development is the increasing integration of Sunday morning adult worship with Christian education for children. Lectionary-based curricula, in which the readings heard in worship form the basis for lessons in Sunday school, are becoming widespread. Many congregations take comfort in knowing that what is happening in worship is also going on in the church school.

Another new development is the practice of intergenerational worship and education, often promoted by lectionary-based curricula. Intergenerational activities celebrate the fact that the church is people *of all ages* who come together for learning and worship. The dramas in *Scripture Out Loud!* are well suited for such settings.

Christian worship and education have traditionally relied upon the use of one person reading while others listen to the words. Some preachers, worship planners, and educators are beginning to use other ways to relate the good news, such as video, audio, interactive media, and visual and performing arts. The dramas in *Scripture Out Loud!* can be used as an alternative to convey scripture readings during worship.

The twelve short, low-stress, high-impact readings and dramas in *Scripture Out Loud!* harmonize smoothly with many styles of worship and diverse church programs. Whether you are just getting started in liturgical drama, or you have a polished drama team already in place, we hope that *Scripture Out Loud!* is a resource your congregation will turn to again and again.

User-friendly drama

Each drama in *Scripture Out Loud!* was written to work in several different, *easy* ways. Many can be used effectively as multi-part readings—without costumes, scenery, props, or much staging. If you are more comfortable starting out slowly, you might want to try this staged reading approach first.

For those who want to take advantage of the impact of drama, but have a small budget and no available costumes or props, simple instructions are given in the section called "Notes for Church School/Youth Leaders and Worship Team" preceding each play. But, please, be kind to yourself. An inordinate amount of time and energy can be spent making elaborate costumes and building sets. If you are feeling overwhelmed, ask yourself if a particular item enhances the key message in the drama. If it does not, it is expendable.

If you have a lot of experience in church drama, as well as sophisticated lighting, scenery and props, you can use the staging ideas in *Scripture Out Loud!* as a starting point for your own unique productions. You may also choose to link some of the dramas together as acts in a longer play. Performing the last four dramas together, for example, effectively tells the story from Easter Day through the Day of Pentecost. These dramas may also serve as the backbone for midweek Lenten worship—with or without preaching

Calling all actors: age 10 to 100

The dramatic readings in *Scripture Out Loud!* can serve people of all ages—from upper elementary church school classes, to teen groups, to adult worship gatherings.

Children performing *Scripture Out Loud!* dramas will require some adult help. You may want to tell the story to the class first, read through the script together several times, ask and answer questions about the reading, and *then* begin planning the drama. Since many of the dramas take five minutes or less, they can be incorporated into a longer class session or done on the spur of the moment. Children enjoy the spontaneity of acting out dramas, and are usually quite content using odds and ends around the classroom for costumes and props.

Teens may only need background information on the story before performing the *Scripture Out Loud!* dramas. Encourage teens to create their own staging ideas. They may also enjoy proclaiming the message for the younger children in the congregation.

When performing the *Scripture Out Loud!* dramas during worship services, consider using an intergenerational cast as often as possible. Try to look beyond conventional or stereotyped casting; in addition to involving more people in your congregation, it may encourage listeners to think about familiar stories in a fresh way. You may want to involve the listeners further and have the cast move among the congregation. Encourage actors to process throughout the church or auditorium, use listeners as extras in crowd scenes, or have them accompany actors to different stations.

Several dramas include phonetic spelling of words to assist actors with pronunciation. Following is a pronunciation guide (also included on page 62).

syllable:	as in:	syllable:	as in:
ah	water	aw	awe
a	cat	uh	dull
eh	net	ih	sit
ee	feet	ay	day
oh	boat	rr	flipped "r"
oo	boot	ch	soft "ch" sound, like "Bach"

High-impact drama without a high-tech budget

You do not need a large budget to establish a church drama group. Here are a few inexpensive, multi-purpose items you can start collecting.

Fabric: Lengths of fabric can be used as costumes, banners, room dividers, tablecloths, and scenery. Buy 2-yard lengths to drape over children for quick tunics, and 3-yard lengths for adults. Use 2-yard lengths of rope or cord as belts. Choose machine-washable, wrinkle-free fabrics in white, tan, brown, black, and blue. If you sew a 2-inch hem in one end of the fabric, you can insert a dowel rod and hang it for an instant wall. A collection of inexpensive plastic tablecloths in various colors may be helpful for props and scenery, as well.

Lighting: Before purchasing any lighting, experiment with the available lighting in your church or auditorium. Many churches have built-in spotlights on the altar or stage. If you are going to use spotlights frequently, movable track lighting with 2 or 3 fixtures and spotlight bulbs can be purchased at a fairly low cost. In classrooms, clip-on desk lamps or powerful flashlights can be used as spotlights. Make sure that any lights you buy can be easily moved from one location to another and serve as many needs as possible.

Equipment: The only equipment suggested in *Scripture Out Loud!* are a tape recorder, electric fans, and an overhead projector. Many quick and easy special effects can be accomplished using an overhead projector. In the *Scripture Out Loud!* dramas, Jesus appears to sit on a donkey on Passion Sunday, and tongues of fire appear over the disciples' heads on the Day of Pentecost. (Instructions are given in the "Notes for Church School/Youth Leaders and Worship Team.")

Props: *Scripture Out Loud!* incorporates pantomimed action throughout the dramas. Only a few essential props are needed, most of which can be found at home or in church.

That's all there is to it! It is with the goal of communicating the timeless truths of scripture that we dedicate this work to the glory of God. May it be as rewarding for you to use as it was for the authors to prepare.

Copyright permission

This book includes permission to reproduce the scripts and use them in local (not-for-profit) church uses; this permission does not include the introduction to each play. Please be sure to include the copyright acknowledgements found at the bottom of the first page of each script. If you have any questions about this permission or wish to use the plays in another context, please contact the publisher.

The Right Reasons

Matthew 6:1-6, 16-21

Ash Wednesday, Years A B C

Before you begin...

Jesus' teachings in the Gospel According to Matthew set the highest possible ethical standard: "Be perfect, therefore, as your heavenly Father is perfect" (Matt. 5:48).

Rule following, however, is not an end to itself. Rules should not be followed only to impress others, or to receive rewards, or just because we have to. In his criticism of the Pharisees (23:25-28), Jesus calls for unity between the inner and outer person. He condemns those who follow all the rules, yet do not orient their inner lives toward God. In God's eyes, virtuous outward behavior without the right interior motivation is hypocrisy.

In this passage, Jesus explains that the important thing is not *what* we do to express our faith, but *why* we do it. His statement implies that the only acceptable motivation for the practice of religion is sincere devotion to God. If our prayers, charity, and fasting are done for show or for personal gain, then God does not want them.

Our outward behavior, then, must begin in our hearts. As Joel declares in another reading for Ash Wednesday, "Yet even now, says the LORD, return to me with all your heart...rend your hearts and not your clothing" (Joel 2:12). The ethical life to which Jesus calls us in the Gospel of Matthew is not motivated by a desire to follow rules, but by the love of God within.

Duration: 10–12 minutes.

Costumes: regular clothing for all characters except: (SCENE I) blazer/suit coat for Proud Giver, old cardigan sweater for Needy Person; (SCENE III) old cardigan sweater for Grumpy Faster.

Props: camera, microphone, check, wallet with six dollar bills, envelope, box labeled "Mail," Bible, plate of doughnuts, folding chair, towel, trophies in a box, polishing cloth.

Optional props: 2 moveable spotlights.

Stage assistant: 1 person to work spotlights.

Notes for church school/youth leaders and worship team: "The Right Reasons" is the least traditional drama in this book. It juxtaposes scripture passages with contemporary action. The pantomimed vignettes are easy to perform and a lot of fun for actors age 10 and up, male and female. If used in worship, this drama offers a great opportunity to use an intergenerational cast. For church school and youth groups, it offers an opportunity for younger children to perform. Even those too young to fully understand the lectionary reading will learn from the vignettes.

The Right Reasons

Matthew 6:1-6, 16-21

Ash Wednesday, Years A B C

Key message: In this teaching, Jesus appears to be telling us *how* to pray and practice our religion. He is, however, actually teaching us to examine the *reasons* we pray, help the poor, and fast. As we begin the season of Lent, Jesus wants us to be motivated by the right reasons to live out our faith.

Cast: 1 reader, 5 actors to pantomime all roles. (Note: Gender references in the script are used randomly. Either men or women can play all roles.)
SCENE I: Reader, Proud Giver, Photographer, Reporter, Needy Person, Humble Giver.
SCENE II: Reader, Proud Prayer, 3 Admirers, Humble Prayer.
SCENE III: Reader, Grumpy Faster, 3 People with doughnuts, Cheerful Faster.
SCENE IV: Reader, Collector, 2 Family members, 2 Friends.

SCENE I

(Actors get in position: READER at podium. PROUD GIVER, REPORTER, PHOTOGRAPHER at the back of the center aisle or room. NEEDY PERSON stage right. HUMBLE GIVER stage left. Mail box should be placed stage right of HUMBLE GIVER, but out of the way for the first vignette. [If you are using spotlights, direct spotlight 1 toward center stage and direct spotlight 2 stage left, but do not turn on until vignettes take place.])

READER: Jesus taught us that the true value of giving, praying, and worshiping God lies in a sincere desire to do God's will. Those whose motive is the attention and approval of others receive only earthly reward.

About giving. Beware of doing your good deeds in front of others so that they can see you, for then you will have no reward from God in heaven. When you give to those in need, don't sound a trumpet. The proud sound trumpets out in public so that others may praise them. I tell you truly, they have received their reward.

([Turn on spotlight 1.] PROUD GIVER strides up center aisle, nodding and waving to the congregation. PHOTOGRAPHER and REPORTER hurry after him, taking pictures and pushing a microphone toward his face. NEEDY PERSON crosses to center stage. PROUD GIVER waves some more, talks to the REPORTER, and grandly presents the check to NEEDY PERSON. He then puts his arm around her and smiles for the camera. NEEDY PERSON looks embarrassed. FREEZE in place. [Spotlight 1 off.])

READER: When you give to others, do not let your left hand know what your right hand is doing, so that your giving may be done in secret. God in heaven who knows our secrets will reward you.

([Turn on spotlight 2.] HUMBLE GIVER takes out a wallet and removes all her money—six bills. She fans them out and looks at them. Then she takes

two and puts them in an envelope. She looks at the remaining bills, then takes two more and puts them in the envelope and seals it. She crosses right to a mail box, drops the envelope in, then smiles to herself. FREEZE in place. [Spotlight 2 off.])

READER: Let us think for a moment about giving in our own lives.

SCENE II

(Actors get in position: PROUD PRAYER back of the center aisle or room. ADMIRERS seated in second row. HUMBLE PRAYER positions folding chair slightly left of center stage then crosses stage left. [Direct spotlight 1 toward center stage; direct spotlight 2 left of center.])

READER: About praying. When you pray, do not be like the proud. They love to stand and pray in public so that others will see them. Truly I tell you, they have received their reward.

([Turn on spotlight 1.] PROUD PRAYER walks up center aisle to center stage. Using large arm gestures, PROUD PRAYER raises his arms to heaven, then fusses with Bible, praying energetically. ADMIRERS nudge each other and point to PROUD PRAYER, nodding their approval. PROUD PRAYER walks over to his admirers, and encourages them to stand and pray conspicuously. [Follow Proud Prayer with spotlight 1.] FREEZE in place. [Spotlight 1 off.])

READER: But whenever you pray, go into your room and shut the door. Pray to God in secret; and God, who sees in secret, will reward you.

([Turn on spotlight 2.] HUMBLE PRAYER crosses right quietly, pantomimes closing the door, and sits on the chair. She bows her head, folds her hands, and prays quietly. [Spotlight 2 off.])

READER: *(Pause)* Let us take a moment for our own prayers.

SCENE III

(Actors get in position: GRUMPY FASTER seated in chair. Hair and clothes should look a little messed up. CHEERFUL FASTER stage right. PEOPLE WITH DOUGHNUTS stage left. [Direct spotlight 1 left of center stage; direct spotlight 2 right of center.])

READER: About fasting. Whenever you fast, don't look dismal like the hypocrites. They twist their faces in pain to show others that they are fasting. I tell you truly, they have received their reward.

([Turn on spotlight 1.] GRUMPY FASTER stands up, sighs, holds her stomach, sighs again. PEOPLE WITH DOUGHNUTS cross stage right, greet her cheerfully and offer a donut. GRUMPY FASTER sighs, holds on to the chair for strength, looks at the doughnuts, sighs, shakes her head "no." Then she straightens up, gestures that she is fasting, and wags her finger at the others for eating doughnuts during Lent. PEOPLE WITH DOUGHNUTS back up and exchange guilty looks. FREEZE. [Spotlight 1 off.])

READER: But when you fast, comb your hair and wash your face, so that your fasting can't be seen by others, but only by God. And God, who sees your secrets, will reward you.

([Turn on spotlight 2.] CHEERFUL FASTER stands up, combs hair, washes face, straightens clothes. He then crosses toward center stage. PEOPLE WITH DOUGHNUTS approach cautiously. He waves a cheerful "hello." They offer a doughnut. CHEERFUL FASTER smiles, but refuses. The doughnut people walk away happily. CHEERFUL FASTER looks longingly at the doughnuts for a moment, then shrugs and smiles. [Spotlight 2 off.])

READER: Let's take a moment to think about the ways we worship God.

SCENE IV

(Actors get in position: COLLECTOR moves small table center stage, then places the box of trophies on the chair. FRIENDS stage left. FAMILY members stage right. [Direct spotlight 1 toward center stage; direct spotlight 2 left of center.])

READER: About treasures. Do not collect treasures for yourselves on earth. Moths and rust can destroy them, and thieves can break in and steal them.

([Turn on spotlight 1.] COLLECTOR opens box of trophies. He carefully polishes each one and places it in exactly the right spot on the table, smiling in satisfaction. He suddenly realizes that one is missing, and is very upset. FREEZE. [Spotlight 1 off.])

READER: Store up for yourselves treasures in heaven. For there neither moth nor rust can destroy, and thieves cannot break in and steal. Where your treasure is, that's where your heart will be.

([Turn on spotlight 2.] FAMILY members walk slowly toward center stage. FRIENDS walk rapidly toward them, waving and calling. FAMILY waits for FRIENDS, and they greet each other with hugs and animated conversation. Then one points to the upset COLLECTOR, and they all go over and console him, bringing him into the loving group. All turn and face viewers.)

READER: During this sacred season of Lent let us all share the treasure in our hearts.

NOTE: You may want to end the drama with a prayer or song.

Faithful to God

Luke 4:1-13
Lent 1, Year C

Before you begin...

In this reading from the Gospel of Luke, Jesus has recently been baptized by John. God has proclaimed him to be "my Son, the Beloved" (Luke 3:22). The story of Jesus' temptations answers the question of what kind of child Jesus will be. Jesus will be a faithful child of God who is unwavering in his devotion to God. He does not accept the three challenges from the one who embodies the evil that Jesus opposes throughout his ministry.

The first challenge tempts Jesus to exploit his unique relationship with God to satisfy his own needs. Even though he is famished after forty days of fasting, Jesus refuses the devil's offer of bread, and demonstrates his dependence upon God alone to provide for him. It is more important for Jesus to rely totally upon God than to put food in his stomach.

Next, Jesus is tempted to take political power if he will worship the devil. Through his death, resurrection, and ascension, Jesus would eventually have power over all time and space—power that comes only from God. Mere political power, attained at the price of denying God, is not what Jesus has come to earth to achieve.

The last temptation occurs at the temple in Jerusalem, which is the site of Jesus' final confrontation with, and victory over, the devil. Jesus is asked to prove his relationship with God by throwing himself off the pinnacle of the temple and allowing God to rescue him. Jesus knows, however, that he has come, not to save himself or to be saved by God, but to give his life away in obedience to God's will. This, for Jesus, is what being a true son and a true disciple entails.

Duration: 3–4 minutes.

Costumes: a plain neutral-colored robe for Jesus, a robe of a different color or long cape for the devil.

Prop: a large, smooth stone.

Optional props: a strobe light, twinkling white Christmas lights, or other type of dramatic lighting; large oscillating fan; scenery to indicate a mountain and the temple.

Stage assistants: 1 person to work lights and 1 person to work fan.

Notes for church school/youth leaders and worship team: If the physical setup of the performance area permits, Jesus and the devil can walk around the room and through the congregation to give a greater illusion of time and distance.

Faithful to God

Luke 4:1-13

Lent 1, Year C

Key message: In his experience in the wilderness, Jesus shows us who he is and what he stands for. He depends on God alone to meet his needs, he refuses to place anything but God at the center of his life, and he demonstrates that he has come, not to save his life, but to sacrifice it. For Jesus, being God's unique child means placing God's will above his own in all circumstances, no matter what the cost. Through his responses to temptation, Jesus models a life that is faithful to God.

Cast: 3 speaking parts: Narrator, Jesus, Devil.

(Enter JESUS stage left. He prays as he walks. Enter DEVIL stage right.)

NARRATOR: After being baptized by John and filled with the Holy Spirit, Jesus returned from the Jordan. He was led by the Holy Spirit into the wilderness, and was tempted by the devil for forty days. He ate nothing at all during those days, and when they were over, he was famished. And the devil tempted him.

DEVIL: *(picks up the smooth stone and holds it out to JESUS)* If you are the Son of God, command this stone to become a loaf of bread.

JESUS: *(turns away)* It is written in the scripture, "One does not live by bread alone."

NARRATOR: Then the devil led Jesus up to a high place, and showed him in an instant all the nations of the world.

(JESUS and DEVIL walk a short distance.)

DEVIL: To you I will give authority over all nations and their glory. For it has been given to me, and I can give it to anyone I please. All this will be yours if you worship me.

(DEVIL twirls and points outward with a flourish. [Turn on strobe, twinkling lights, or other special effects lighting.])

JESUS: It is written, "Worship the Lord your God, and serve God only."

(JESUS walks away. [Special lighting stops abruptly.] The DEVIL watches for a moment then quickly follows. He grabs JESUS' arm and pulls him in another direction.)

NARRATOR: Then the devil took Jesus to Jerusalem and placed him on the highest point of the temple.

[Turn on fan to its most powerful setting.]

DEVIL: If you are the Son of God, throw yourself down from here. *(DEVIL stretches out arms and cape/robe blows in the wind.)* For it is written, "God will send angels to protect you," and "With their hands they will hold you up, so that you will not even scrape your foot against a stone."

JESUS: *(vehemently)* It is also said, "Do not put the Lord your God to the test!"

([Stop fan.] JESUS kneels and prays.)

NARRATOR: After the devil had tested Jesus in every way, he left until a later time.

(DEVIL watches JESUS pray for a moment, then angrily leaves the stage.)

Now I See

John 9:1-41
Lent 4, Year A

Before you begin...

John's gospel abounds with brilliant irony. In this passage, the primary irony is that the blind man sees, while others who do have their physical vision are blind. John also makes frequent use of metaphor. In this chapter, *sight* and *blindness* are metaphors for the ability, or inability, to know God as revealed in Jesus. In addition to having his sight restored, the blind man comes to believe that Jesus is the Messiah. While others remain blind to the truth of Jesus, the blind man sees both physically and spiritually.

This passage also addresses the nature of sin. The Pharisees, and even the disciples, are convinced that the man's blindness is a result of someone's sin—either the man's or his parents'. In biblical times many believed that illness resulted from a moral lapse on the part of the affected person, or his or her parents. The Pharisees' strict interpretation of the law led them to believe that Jesus has sinned by making mud and healing the man on the Sabbath, the day of rest.

In John's gospel, however, sin is not merely a matter of what you do or fail to do. Sin is the unwillingness to see God in Jesus and believe that Jesus is the Messiah. Sin is a breach in the relationship with God. As Jesus points out, "neither this man nor his parents sinned" (John 9:3). Rather, his condition presents an opportunity for God's grace to be revealed. By the end of the story, those presumed to be sinners—the man and Jesus—are shown to be sinless. It is those who fail to see that light and life are found through faith in Jesus who are caught up in sin.

Duration: 5–7 minutes.

Costumes: plain robes or tunics for men, robes and headpieces for women, 2 expensive-looking robes for Pharisees.

Props: bench, begging bowl.

Optional prop: moveable spotlight.

Stage assistant: 1 person to work spotlight.

Notes for church school/youth leaders and worship team: This drama is not difficult to perform, but it has a lot of movement. You will need to define three separate performance areas: the blind man's bench/neighborhood, the pool of Siloam, and the temple. The action goes from the bench to Siloam, then back to the bench, then to the temple, and then back to the bench. Actors should be able to enter and exit both stage left and stage right.

Now I See

John 9:1-41
Lent 4, Year A

Key message: Jesus is the light of the world. He came to earth to give those who are spiritually blind the opportunity to see—to know him and the God who sent him. Just as the blind man came to see and know Jesus and the God who sent him, we too, by faith in Jesus, are restored to a right relationship with God.

Cast: 10 speaking, (3 nonspeaking): Blind man, Narrator, Disciple 1, (2 other disciples), Jesus, Neighbor 1, Neighbor 2, Neighbor 3, Pharisee 1, Pharisee 2, Blind man's father, (Blind man's mother).

(BLIND MAN is sitting on the bench. He hears people approaching and holds out his begging bowl.)

BLIND MAN: Alms for the poor! Have pity on a poor blind man!

(Enter JESUS and his DISCIPLES. The DISCIPLES point to BLIND MAN and whisper among themselves.)

NARRATOR: As Jesus and his disciples walked along, they saw a man who was blind from birth. The disciples wondered whether the man's blindness was a punishment for sins committed by him or his parents, as was commonly believed in Jesus' time.

DISCIPLE: Teacher, why was this man born blind? Did he or his parents sin?

JESUS: *(stops and turns to BLIND MAN)* Neither this man nor his parents sinned. *(pause)* But you will see God's works revealed through his blindness, for I am the light of the world.

NARRATOR: After he said this he spat on the ground and made mud with his saliva. He spread the mud on the man's eyes.

(JESUS crouches and pantomimes making mud, which he spreads gently on the man's eyes.)

JESUS: *(rises and helps BLIND MAN stand)* Go, wash in the pool of Siloam (sih-LOH-ahm).

(BLIND MAN walks to the stage area that represents Siloam. JESUS and DISCIPLES exit. BLIND MAN pantomimes washing his face with water from the pool. [Spotlight on man.] His eyes open, and he looks around in amazement. Then he slowly starts walking back toward the bench. [Spotlight follows him.] Enter THREE NEIGHBORS who stop and watch him.)

NEIGHBOR 1: *(nudges NEIGHBOR 2)* Isn't that the blind man who used to sit and beg?

NEIGHBOR 2: Yes, that's him.

NEIGHBOR 3: No, it's just someone who looks like him.

BLIND MAN: *(turning to them)* Yes! I am the man.

NEIGHBOR 1: Then how were your eyes opened?

BLIND MAN: The man called Jesus made mud, spread it on my eyes, and said to go to Siloam and wash. So I went and washed the mud from my eyes and received my sight.

NEIGHBOR 2: *(looking around)* Where is this man Jesus? Where did he go?

BLIND MAN: *(looking around)* I don't know.

> *(NEIGHBORS gather around BLIND MAN and take him to PHARISEES who enter from the far end of the stage area. [Spotlight off.])*

NARRATOR: They brought the man who had been blind to the Pharisees. Now the Pharisees were a powerful group of educated religious leaders who studied the Hebrew law, and demanded that the people obey the law down to the smallest detail. It was a Sabbath day when Jesus made the mud and opened the blind man's eyes, and by law no work could be done on the Sabbath. So the Pharisees asked the man how he had received his sight, to see if Jesus had violated the law.

BLIND MAN: He put mud on my eyes. Then I washed, and now I see.

PHARISEE 1: *(to second PHARISEE)* This man, Jesus, cannot be from God, for he does not observe the Sabbath.

PHARISEE 2: How can a man who is a sinner perform such signs?

> *(The PHARISEES argue quietly with each other.)*

NARRATOR: And they were divided in their opinions.

PHARISEE 1: *(turning to BLIND MAN)* What do you say about Jesus? It was your eyes he opened.

BLIND MAN: He is a prophet.

> *(The PHARISEES reject his reply. They order the BLIND MAN'S PARENTS brought to them. The NEIGHBORS exit and return with the PARENTS, who are clearly frightened.)*

NARRATOR: The Pharisees did not believe that the man had really been blind and then received his sight. So they sent for his parents and questioned them.

PHARISEE 2: *(to FATHER)* Is this your son who you say was born blind? How is it he can suddenly see?

FATHER: This is our son, and he was born blind. But we don't know why he can see now, nor do we know who opened his eyes. Ask him; he's an adult. He can speak for himself.

PHARISEE 1: *(turning to BLIND MAN)* Give glory to God! We know that this man Jesus is a sinner.

BLIND MAN: I don't know whether or not he's a sinner. But one thing I do know: I was blind, and now I see.

(PHARISEES confer with each other.)

PHARISEE 2: What exactly did he do to you? How did he open your eyes?

BLIND MAN: *(exasperated)* I have told you already, but you wouldn't listen! Why do *you* want to hear it again? Do *you* want to become his disciples?

PHARISEE 2: *(angrily)* You are his disciple, but we are disciples of Moses. We know that God has spoken to Moses, but as for this man—we don't know where he comes from!

BLIND MAN: *(sarcastically)* What an astonishing thing! You don't know where Jesus comes from, and yet he opened my eyes. Never since the world began, have the eyes of a person born blind been opened. If this man were not from God, he could do nothing!

PHARISEE 1: You were born a sinner, yet you think you can teach us? Be gone from here!

(BLIND MAN, NEIGHBORS, and PARENTS all walk away from the Pharisees. All exit stage except the BLIND MAN. He sits on the bench and looks thoughtfully at his begging bowl.)

NARRATOR: Jesus heard that they had driven the blind man out of the temple, and went and found him.

(Enter JESUS.)

JESUS: Do you believe in the Son of Man?

BLIND MAN: *(looking up)* Who is he, sir? Tell me so that I may believe in him.

JESUS: You have seen him. He's the one you're speaking with. *[Spotlight on JESUS and BLIND MAN.]*

BLIND MAN: Lord, I believe. *(BLIND MAN falls on his knees in front of JESUS.)*

(PHARISEES enter and stand to the side listening, outside range of spotlight.)

JESUS: I came into this world to give sight to the blind—and to make blind those who think they see.

PHARISEE 1: Surely we are not blind, are we?

JESUS: *(to PHARISEES)* If you were truly blind, you would not be guilty. But since you say, "We can see," your sin remains.

(PHARISEES angrily exit stage right. JESUS and BLIND MAN slowly exit stage left while talking.)

Salvation's Hope

Mark 11:1-11
Passion/Palm Sunday, Year B

Before you begin...

We know how the story will turn out. We know that the crowd of well-wishers in this passage will be the same crowd that, just a few days later, demands Jesus' execution (Mark 15:13). We know that Jesus is soon to undergo the humiliating suffering and death that he came to earth to accomplish. It is nearly impossible to hear these happy verses without thinking of the ominous events that are about to transpire. That is why Palm Sunday is also called Passion Sunday.

The many people who honor Jesus as he rides on the donkey are among the thousands who, like Jesus and the disciples, are journeying to Jerusalem to celebrate Passover. Though they may have heard about Jesus, the miracle-working teacher from Galilee, they are probably not his followers. The scene recalls the entrance processions of messianic figures of old; it is doubtful, however, that this crowd regards Jesus as the Messiah.

It is certain that those who spread cloaks and leafy branches on the road have high hopes for salvation and deliverance. That is, after all, the promise of Passover. In some way they connect their hopes with Jesus, and welcome this fellow traveler as a representative of God. They are eager to follow anyone who seems to embody their desires for spiritual and political renewal. For the moment, Jesus is their man.

Even if some in the crowd believe Jesus is the Messiah, they cannot possibly imagine the kind of Messiah he will prove to be in the week ahead. In the popular imagination, the Messiah will bring the reign of God with fantastic displays of power and might, destroying the tyranny of Rome and restoring the Davidic dynasty. The Messiah that Jesus turns out to be, however, is one whose power is revealed in willing suffering and sacrifice. The masses do not accept this kind of Messiah.

Duration: 3 minutes for drama, 5 minutes for procession.

Costumes: plain white robe or tunic for Jesus, plain robes or tunics for all other participants, 2 coats/shawls for the disciples, headdresses for women.

Props: palms or similar branches, extra shawls and coats for people in the crowd, tall stool, overhead projector, one transparency, construction paper for arch and donkey (see "Notes for church school/youth leaders and worship team"), taped or live music.

Stage assistant: 1 person to work overhead projector and taped music.

Notes for church school/youth leaders and worship team: This drama has more props than usual, but they are not complicated. Large pieces of fabric can be used as the clothing that is placed on the road. If you do not have enough costumes, you can drape fabric around cast members and secure it with rope or belts. Make sure you have enough palms for the entire congregation, since they will be invited to participate in the procession at the end of the drama.

To make the arch and donkey illusions: Cut out an arch shape from a piece of paper that is large enough to cover the entire lighted surface of the projector. The arch should be about 7 inches high and 5 inches wide. Lightly tape the paper to the surface of the overhead projector. Draw the side profile of a donkey, or find a photo of one that fits in the paper arch. Cut it out and paste it onto a blank transparency. Project the arch onto the wall before the drama starts. The image should be tall enough to look life-size. Have an assistant slowly move the donkey transparency into the archway as the disciples bring the donkey to Jesus. When Jesus sits on the tall stool in front of the image, he should look like he's sitting on the donkey.

Salvation's Hope

Mark 11:1-11

Passion/Palm Sunday, Year B

Key message: Jesus is welcomed on the road to Jerusalem as a special messenger of God. We, too, gladly welcome Jesus in our lives, with hope for divine renewal. Let us live our lives following in the way of Jesus—the way of the cross—and receive him as the hope of our salvation.

Cast: 6 speaking, (1 nonspeaking): Narrator, Jesus, Bystander, Disciple 1, (Disciple 2), Voice 1 in crowd, Voice 2 in crowd, Crowd.

(JESUS and DISCIPLES enter stage left.)

NARRATOR: As Jesus and his disciples approached Jerusalem, near the Mount of Olives, Jesus sent two of his disciples on ahead.

JESUS: Go into the village ahead of you. As soon as you enter town you will find a young donkey that has never been ridden. Untie it and bring it to me. If anyone asks what you're doing, just say, "The Lord needs it and will return it very soon."

(DISCIPLES cross stage right. BYSTANDER enters stage right. DISCIPLES pantomime finding and untying donkey.)

NARRATOR: The disciples went off and found a young donkey tied up outside in the street, near a door. As they were untying it, a person standing nearby challenged them.

BYSTANDER: Hey, what are you doing? Why are you untying that donkey?

DISCIPLE: The Lord needs it and will return it very soon.

BYSTANDER: All right, take it.

(DISCIPLES pantomime leading donkey back to JESUS. [Move silhouette of donkey into the archway. The stool should be positioned in front of the silhouette, so that Jesus will appear to be sitting on the donkey.])

NARRATOR: The disciples brought the donkey to Jesus. They covered the donkey with their coats, and Jesus sat on it. Many people spread their clothes on the road, and others cut leafy branches in the fields and spread those on the road. Then those who went ahead of Jesus and those who followed began to shout.

(DISCIPLES drape cloaks over the stool. JESUS sits on stool. Some in CROWD begin to lay a path of clothes and palms toward congregation.)

CROWD: Hosanna! Hosanna!

(CROWD members wave palms.)

VOICE 1 IN CROWD: Blessed is the one who comes in the name of the Lord!

VOICE 2 IN CROWD: Blessed is the coming kingdom of our ancestor David!

CROWD: Hosanna in the highest heaven! Hosanna! Hosanna!

(If the congregation does not customarily participate in a processional liturgy on this day the following is offered as an alternative.

PROCESSION: An instrumental introduction to a Palm Sunday hymn begins ("All Glory, Laud, and Honor," "Ride On, Ride On in Majesty," or "Lift Up Your Hearts, O Gates"). CAST starts singing and processes into congregation distributing palms and encouraging others to join them. JESUS slips off stool and walks near front of the procession. Process for remainder of song. Exit CAST; others return to their seats.)

True Love

John 13:1-17, 31b-35

Maundy Thursday, Years A B C

Before you begin...

Jesus' hour has come. It is time for him to complete his work of revealing God's love by his own loving words and deeds. Gathered around the table with his disciples on the night before his death, Jesus demonstrates the full extent of his love by washing his disciples' feet.

In biblical times, people typically washed their feet upon returning home after a long, dusty journey. When entering the house of another person, the host's servant often washed the guest's feet. Foot washing was thus associated with the hospitality and service shown to an honored person.

Therefore it would have been proper for the disciples to wash Jesus' feet in deference to him as their teacher. What surprises us—and Peter—is that Jesus turns the tables and washes *their* feet.

By willingly performing the work of a servant, Jesus shows us God's love and helps us understand the meaning of his actions the next day on the cross. Around the table that night, Jesus gives himself away in loving service to his friends. On the cross, he will give himself away for all. Peter is invited to have his feet washed, thereby entering into an intimate relationship with Jesus. We are also invited to receive the self-giving love Jesus offers on the cross, and be in relationship with him and the God who sent him.

In addition to demonstrating God's love, the foot washing is a model for Christian servanthood: "So if I, your Lord and Teacher, have washed your feet, you also ought to wash one another's feet" (John 13:14). As Jesus shows love through humble service and giving himself away in death, so we also ought to love others. "I give you a new commandment, that you love one another" (13:34). *Maundy* is from the Latin word for *commandment*. On Maundy Thursday, we recall Jesus' acts of love and his commandment to love each other as he loved us.

Duration: 5–7 minutes.

Costumes: tunic and outer robe for Jesus, simple tunics or robes for the disciples, or contemporary clothing of various occupations or cultures (See "Notes for church school/youth leaders and worship team"), nondescript clothing for Judas.

Props: folding chairs or benches to seat 13, several white bath towels, basin, pitcher, water, low table (such as a coffee table), food for the table—including bread and a wine cup.

Optional prop: background music.

Notes for church school/youth leaders and worship team: This drama has more action than dialogue and, ideally, uses 14 actors. Church school/youth groups may want to invite other classes to join them, or you may choose to use this drama at an intergenerational gathering. The nonspeaking roles do not need to be rehearsed ahead of time.

When used as part of worship, a traditional, all-adult male cast may be used; however, several alternatives may have more impact. Twelve men, women, and teens, dressed in the clothing of diverse occupations—or cultures—could portray the disciples. For example, your cast could include a businessperson, a police officer or firefighter, a farmer or rancher, a waiter, a construction worker, a student, a parent or grandparent, and a healthcare professional. Peter could be a commercial fisherman in a slicker and boots. Likewise, ethnic costumes from around the world beautifully convey the universal aspect of discipleship. Jesus should wear the traditional tunic, robe, and sandals as a contrast to the rest of the cast.

Background music, played while Jesus is washing feet and no dialogue takes place, would be a nice touch. Settings of "Ubi Caritas" or "Where Charity and Love Prevail" might be used. If time is a consideration, Jesus can simply touch the feet with his towel.

True Love

John 13:1-17, 31b-35
Maundy Thursday, Years A B C

Key message: Jesus washes the feet of his disciples to show them—and us—the meaning of his impending death on the cross. As he demonstrates his love for the disciples by washing their feet, so his humiliating death demonstrates his love for us and his desire to be in a close relationship with us. This is the love we ought to have for one another—true love shown in humble service.

Cast: 3 speaking, (11 nonspeaking): Narrator, Jesus, Peter, (Judas), (10 Disciples).

(The chairs or benches are set up in a semi-circle. The low table is several feet in front of the chairs. JESUS sits in the center chair, praying. The basin and towels are by his feet. One by one, 10 DISCIPLES, PETER, and JUDAS enter and are seated. If the cast is dressed in contemporary clothes [see "Notes for church school/youth leaders and worship team"], have them enter rather slowly. They should smile and greet each other—except for JUDAS who remains aloof throughout.)

NARRATOR: It was the time of the Passover festival, and Jesus knew that the hour had come to leave this world and go to the Father. The devil had already put into the heart of Judas, son of Simon Iscariot (ihs-KEHR-ee-aht), the thought of betraying Jesus. Jesus had always loved his disciples in this world, and he loved them now at the very end.

(JESUS rises and greets the DISCIPLES affectionately, then returns to his chair.)

NARRATOR: Jesus knew that all power had been placed into his hands. He had come from the Father and would return to the Father. Before supper, he got up from the table, took off his outer robe, and wrapped a towel around himself.

(JESUS rises, takes off his outer robe, and wraps a towel around himself.)

NARRATOR: Then he poured water into a basin and began to wash the disciples' feet, and to wipe them with the towel that was tied around him.

([Begin background music.] JESUS pours water into the basin. He gestures to several DISCIPLES to remove their footwear. He then briefly washes and dries their feet. PETER leans forward and watches in disbelief as JESUS moves closer to where he is sitting.)

NARRATOR: He came to Simon Peter, who wondered what he was doing.

PETER: Lord, are you going to wash my feet?

JESUS: You don't know now what I am doing, but later you will understand.

PETER: You will never wash my feet!

JESUS: Unless I wash you, you can no longer be my disciple.

PETER: *(quickly pulls off shoes)* Lord, wash not only my feet, but my hands and my face, too!

JESUS: One who has bathed is entirely clean and does not need to wash, except for the feet. And you are all clean *(looks at JUDAS)*—except for one.

(JUDAS scowls and looks away. The other DISCIPLES look at each other in confusion.)

NARRATOR: Jesus said this because he knew Judas was to betray him.

(JESUS finishes washing all feet, then returns to his chair and puts his outer robe back on.)

NARRATOR: After he had washed all his disciples' feet, he put on his robe and returned to the table. Then he explained his actions to them.

JESUS: Do you understand what I have done to you? You call me Teacher and Lord—and you are right, for that is what I am. So if I, your Lord and Teacher, have washed your feet, you then, should wash one another's feet. I have set an example for you—do as I have done to you.

(Some of the DISCIPLES start washing each other's feet.)

JESUS: I tell you truly, servants are not greater than their master, nor are messengers greater than the one who sent them. If you believe these things and do as I say, God will bless you. The Son of Man will be glorified, and God will be glorified through him.

(JESUS gathers the DISCIPLES closer to him. JUDAS remains seated.)

JESUS: My children, I will be with you only a little while longer. You will look for me, but what I have told the people I say now to you: "Where I am going, you cannot come." I give you a new commandment, that you love one another just as I have loved you. If you do this, if you have love for one another, then everyone will know that you are my disciples.

(JESUS starts to hug the DISCIPLES, who in turn hug each other. Actors slowly exit the stage area. Depending on when the drama is used, the Holy Communion liturgy may follow.)

It Is Finished

John 18:1—19:42 Abridged
Good Friday, Years A B C

Before you begin...

As the letters of Paul make clear, Jesus' death and resurrection formed the core proclamation of the early church. All four gospels build to this grand conclusion. Many churches traditionally hear the entire passion twice—on Passion Sunday and Good Friday. What are we to make of this vast and vital story?

Differing somewhat from the other gospels, John's gospel makes it clear that Jesus goes to the cross in complete willingness. Jesus is sent by God to give his life away for the sake of the world. In this gospel, Jesus' death is not so much a murder as it is self-sacrifice made in utter obedience to God's will. "No one takes [my life] from me, but I lay it down of my own accord" (John 10:18). The other gospels portray Jesus as a victim, overtaken by the events that lead to his death. On one level of John's gospel, Jesus *appears* to be controlled by those who betray, seize, deny, brutalize, try, and crucify him. Upon closer inspection, however, it becomes clear that he is in supreme control of every aspect of his hour. He is already a victor over death.

During the arrest, Peter cuts off the ear of the high priest's slave. Jesus commands Peter to stop the violence, asking, "Am I not to drink the cup that the Father has given me?" (18:11). Jesus has come to this hour by his own choice, and in obedience to God. Nothing, including Peter's retaliation against Jesus' opponents, can stop the progression of events.

In contrast to Peter's cowardly denials, Jesus responds boldly to Annas (18:20-21). His impudent behavior and stubborn witness to the truth earn him a blow from the police. It almost seems that he *wants* to go on to the next step in the process, which is a trial before Pilate.

The contrast between Pilate and Jesus is remarkable. Jesus is calm and sure, knowing that he will offer himself freely for the salvation of the world. Pilate, on the other hand, scurries between Jesus inside the headquarters and the Jews outside, wondering how he can protect his own interests. In the dialogue between Pilate and Jesus, it is unclear who is questioning whom and who is judging whom. Pilate has nominal control of the proceedings, but we know by Jesus' unashamed words and deeds who is really in charge. Because he comes from God, Jesus is the true king, not Caesar.

With his crucifixion, Jesus reveals once and for all that he is a king who serves by offering his life. In John's narrative, Jesus is depicted as serene and purposeful throughout his ordeal. Nothing is chaotic or frenzied. There is no earthquake. The temple curtain is not torn. Bodies do not rise from their graves. Instead, Jesus willingly carries his own cross. As he hangs on it, rather than uttering a cry of divine abandonment, he says simply, "It is finished" (19:30). Jesus' act of self-giving has achieved the purpose for which he has come—to illustrate to all that he is the light of the world, and be reconciled to the God who sent him.

Duration: 10 minutes.

Costumes: dark, rich-looking robes for Annas, Priest, Joseph of Arimathea, and Nicodemus, white tunic with gold trim and a laurel wreath for Pilate, short tunics, swords, and chest and back armor for soldiers, white tunic and robe for Jesus, plain neutral-colored tunics or robes for all others, sword for Peter.

Props: lantern, 4 swords, rope, sound of cock crowing, rope whip, grapevine wreath for the crown of thorns, purple cape, small chair with arms (such as a dining room chair), lightweight cross, sign with the letters "INRI" printed on it, robe with dirt and red stains, spear, sponge, white shroud, bottle for spices, large cardboard or plywood "rock."

Optional props: stand for the cross, spotlight, scenery if moving to different stations.

Stage assistant: 1 person to work spotlight.

Notes for church school/youth leaders and worship team: Although the story is straightforward and familiar, it is a complex drama to perform. The cast is large and the action takes place at four locations.

If the drama will be used in worship, allow extra rehearsal time. It is easiest to use four different stations within the church or auditorium. If this is not possible, directions have been included in the script for symbolic movement between scenes. Depending on the size and shape of your chancel or stage area, you may want to devise your own way of showing time and distance.

If the play is being used in church school, you might want to consider using only the last two scenes. Once the children know the story they can ad-lib most of the action. They may also enjoy making the props, many of which are traditional Lenten symbols. An intergenerational performance might be helpful for children; they can participate without being overwhelmed by the length and intricacy of the story.

Another consideration is children's reaction to the violence and suffering inflicted on Jesus. In liturgical time, Jesus, who started out as a cuddly Christmas baby, became teacher, healer, and the honored Lord of Passion Sunday in just a few months. Now he is being executed. Explaining the political situation and the jealously guarded power of the religious authorities may help young people understand that Jesus was killed by a small group of enemies, not by the Jewish people—or God.

It Is Finished

John 18:1—19:42 Abridged
Good Friday, Years A B C

Key message: God sent Jesus to bring us to God. Jesus' death completes this mission. "It is finished" does not mean that Jesus failed in his work, though his death may make it appear so. On the contrary, Jesus' work of demonstrating God's love for all is accomplished by his willing death on the cross. Because of what Jesus has done, we are restored to relationship with God.

Cast: 15–16 speaking, (5 nonspeaking): Narrator, Jesus, Peter, Disciple, (Judas), Soldier 1, Soldier 2, (Soldier 3), Priest, Servant, Annas, Woman guard, Bystander, Pilate, Crowd of 3 or 4, (Mary), (Joseph of Arimathea), (Nicodemus).

SCENE I

(JESUS, PETER, and DISCIPLE enter from stage right. They are talking quietly among themselves and stop center stage.)

NARRATOR: Jesus went out with his disciples to a garden called Gethsemene (gehth-SEHM-ah-nee). Now Judas, who betrayed him, knew of this place because Jesus often met there with his disciples. So Judas brought a detachment of soldiers, and they came with lanterns and torches and weapons.

(THREE SOLDIERS, PRIEST, SERVANT, and JUDAS enter noisily from stage left, saying things like "Find him," "Where is he?" etc.)

JESUS: *(coming forward)* Who are you looking for?

SOLDIER 1: Jesus of Nazareth.

JESUS: I am he.

(PETER draws his sword and strikes the high priest's SERVANT's ear.)

JESUS: Put your sword away. Am I not to drink from the cup that I've been given?

(PETER falls back, confused. SOLDIERS grab JESUS and tie his hands behind him. ALL walk counterclockwise in a full circle around the stage to symbolize movement to another place, or move to the next station, as the NARRATOR speaks. JESUS, PRIEST, DISCIPLE, SERVANT, and SOLDIERS stop stage right. PETER stops stage left.)

SCENE II

NARRATOR: So the soldiers arrested Jesus and bound him. First they took him to Annas, father-in-law of the high priest Caiaphas (KAY-ah-fihs). Simon Peter and another disciple followed Jesus. That disciple went with Jesus into the courtyard, for he knew the high priest, but Peter remained outside at the gate. The other disciple spoke to the woman who guarded the gate, then brought Peter in.

(WOMAN enters stage right. DISCIPLE goes up to her and gestures toward PETER. They walk over to PETER.)

WOMAN: *(to PETER)* You are not also one of this man Jesus' disciples, are you?

PETER: *(looking frightened)* No, I'm not.

(The three walk center stage. WOMAN exits. DISCIPLE walks back toward JESUS. PETER warms his hands over an imaginary fire. ANNAS enters stage right and pantomimes speaking with JESUS.)

NARRATOR: The high priest questioned Jesus about his disciples and about his teaching.

JESUS: *(to ANNAS)* I have spoken openly to the world. I have always taught in synagogues and in the temple, where all the Hebrews come together. I have said nothing in secret. Why do you ask me? Ask those who heard me; they know what I said.

SOLDIER 1: *(slaps JESUS' face)* Show some respect for the high priest!

NARRATOR: Meanwhile, Peter was standing in the courtyard, warming himself by a fire.

(Enter BYSTANDER.)

BYSTANDER: *(peers at PETER suspiciously)* Are you also one of Jesus' disciples?

PETER: No! I'm not.

BYSTANDER: Didn't I see you in the garden with him?

PETER: No! You're wrong. I wasn't there!

(Two SOLDIERS pass with JESUS. DISCIPLE, PRIEST, and BYSTANDER follow. ALL walk clockwise in a full circle around the stage. A cock crows. PETER drops to his knees and covers his face in shame, then follows others at a distance.)

SCENE III

NARRATOR: Jesus was taken to Pilate's headquarters.

(CROWD enter and join group. ALL wait stage left. SOLDIER #3 brings in chair and places it right of center. Enter PILATE stage right.)

PILATE: *(goes out to them and looks JESUS up and down)* What accusation do you bring against this man?

PRIEST: This man is a criminal. That's why we have brought him to you.

PILATE: Take him yourselves and judge him according to your law.

PRIEST: We are not permitted to put anyone to death.

(PILATE goes back inside and sits down. JESUS and SOLDIERS follow and stand right of center. PILATE summons JESUS.)

PILATE: Are you the King of the Jews?

JESUS: Do you ask this yourself, or did others tell you about me?

PILATE: I am not a Jew, am I? Your own nation and the chief priests have handed you over to me. What have you done?

JESUS: My kingdom is not in this world. If my kingdom were in this world, my followers would be fighting to keep me from being handed over to the authorities.

PILATE: So you are a king?

JESUS: You say that I am a king. *(pause)* I was born and came into the world to testify to the truth. Everyone who belongs to the truth listens to my voice.

PILATE: What is truth? *(He stares at JESUS for a moment then goes back out to the crowd.)* I find no case against him. But you have a custom that I release someone for you at the Passover. Do you want me to release the King of the Jews?

PRIEST: No, not this man Jesus. Give us the bandit Barabbas (bah-RAB-uhs)!

(PILATE shakes his head, goes back inside, and sits down. He pantomimes orders to SOLDIERS.)

NARRATOR: Then Pilate took Jesus and had him flogged, and the soldiers wove a crown of thorns and put it on his head.

(SOLDIERS pantomime flogging JESUS. They push him around roughly, and put the crown of thorns on his head and a purple cape over his shoulders. PILATE watches.)

SOLDIER 2: *(mockingly bows)* Hail, King of the Jews! *(He strikes JESUS' face. The other soldiers laugh.)*

(PILATE goes back out to the crowd.)

PILATE: Look, I am bringing him out to you to let you know that I find no case against him. *(JESUS comes out wearing the crown of thorns and purple robe.)* Look at the man!

CROWD: Crucify him! Crucify him!

PILATE: Take him yourself and crucify him; I find no case against him.

CROWD: Crucify him! Crucify him!

PRIEST: We have a law, and according to that law, he should die because he has claimed to be the Son of God.

CROWD: *(louder)* Crucify him! Crucify him!

(PILATE draws back looking frightened. He enters his quarters again, followed by SOLDIERS and JESUS.)

PILATE: *(to JESUS)* Where are you from? *(JESUS does not answer.)* Do you refuse to speak to me? Do you not know that I have power to release you, and power to crucify you?

JESUS: You would have no power over me unless it had been given you from above. The one who handed me over to you is guilty of a greater sin.

(PILATE becomes angry and returns to the crowd. SOLDIERS remove purple cape and put torn dirty robe on JESUS. They drag JESUS to where the CROWD can see him.)

PILATE: Here is your king!

CROWD: Away with him! Crucify him!

PILATE: Shall I crucify your king?

PRIEST: We have no king but Caesar.

NARRATOR: And Pilate handed him over to them to be crucified.

(PILATE gestures to the SOLDIERS. They get the cross and put it on JESUS' back. The chair is quietly removed. ALL process counterclockwise in full circle around the stage. MARY enters and joins the group.)

SCENE IV

NARRATOR: So they took Jesus away. He carried the cross by himself, and they went out to the place called Golgotha (GAWL-guh-thah), and there they crucified him along with two others. *(Lean cross against wall, or place in stand. JESUS' outer robe is removed. He stands in front of the cross with arms outstretched.)* Pilate had an inscription put on the cross. It read, "Jesus of Nazareth, the King of the Jews." *(SOLDIER 3 attaches sign to cross.)* After the soldiers had crucified Jesus, they gambled to see who would get his coat. *(SOLDIERS pantomime discussion, and SOLDIER 1 takes bloody robe.)* When Jesus saw his mother, and the disciple whom he loved standing beside her, he spoke.

(MARY and DISCIPLE move toward JESUS.)

JESUS: *(looking at MARY)* Woman, here is your son. *(looking at his DISCIPLE)* Here is your mother. *(pause) (whispers)* I am thirsty.

(SOLDIER 1 puts a sponge full of wine on his spear and holds it to his mouth.)

JESUS: It is finished. *(JESUS bows his head and closes his eyes.)*

(House lights should be turned down. All quietly exit except JESUS and SOLDIER 2. Spotlight on JESUS.)

NARRATOR: The religious authorities did not want any bodies left on crosses during the Sabbath, so they asked Pilate to hurry death by breaking the men's legs. But when they came to Jesus, they saw that he was already dead, so they did not break his legs. One of the soldiers pierced Jesus' side with a spear, and at once blood and water came out. *(Pause as SOLDIER 2 touches JESUS' side with spear.)*

(Enter PILATE who stands far stage right. Enter JOSEPH OF ARIMATHEA, SERVANT, and NICODEMUS from left carrying cloth and bottle of spices. They walk toward PILATE as NARRATOR speaks. JOSEPH speaks to PILATE who nods and exits.)

NARRATOR: Afterward, Joseph of Arimathea (EHR-ih-mah-THEE-ah) asked Pilate to let him take away Jesus' body. Nicodemus (nihk-oh-DEE-muhs) also came, bringing a mixture of myrrh and aloes. They took the body of Jesus and wrapped it with the spices in linen cloths, according to the burial custom of the Hebrews.

(JOSEPH, NICODEMUS, and SOLDIER 2 take JESUS from the cross and lie him on the ground. SOLDIER exits. JOSEPH and NICODEMUS pour on spices and wrap JESUS' body gently in white shroud.)

NARRATOR: There was a garden with a new tomb in the place where Jesus was crucified. Because it was the Jewish day of Preparation, they laid Jesus there.

(SERVANT slowly pushes rock in front of JESUS' body. JOSEPH, SERVANT, and NICODEMUS exit. [Spotlight fades.]).

God's World

Genesis 1:1—2:4a
Easter Vigil, Years A B C

Before you begin...

The first chapter of the Bible seems to be about the creation of the world. Like the rest of the Bible, though, it is really about God. God speaks, God acts, and the result is "good." It also shows us that the Creator is good. The first chapter of Genesis is a hymn of praise and thanks to God who creates life from chaos, and whose intention for life is goodness.

While the creation is wholly God's deed, the world is purposely left unfinished, and is given the responsibility of participating in its own ongoing creation. "Let the earth put forth vegetation" (Gen. 1:11). "Let the earth bring forth living creatures" (1:24). "Let [humankind] have dominion over the fish of the sea, and over the birds of the air...and over every creeping thing" (1:26). Creation, while fundamentally good, is in need of continuing restoration. The creatures themselves, especially human beings, are given the obligation to care for creation. With this responsibility comes the possibility that they may act for its destruction.

God did not make the world as a watchmaker makes a watch. The earth is not a lifeless thing that will run itself flawlessly while the maker looks on. Rather, intending that the world would relate to its creator in gratitude and trust, God designed a dynamic and free creation. Far from being a God who creates and commands from afar, our God has sought an intimate relationship with us from the beginning—sharing, interacting, trusting, inviting, and moving us along.

The divine-human partnership for the renewal of creation comes to full fruition in Jesus Christ. For centuries, Christian poets have noted that the creation of humankind was accomplished on the afternoon of the sixth day, Friday—the very time when Jesus died on the cross. It may be said, then, that what God began at the beginning of history, God finished in the passion of Christ. Just as God created life out of chaos, God redeems life out of the chaos of the cross. Thanks to Jesus' death and resurrection, God's original creation—already good—is becoming the new creation that God intended all along.

Duration: 5 minutes without special effects; 6–8 minutes with audio or visual props.

Costumes: None.

Notes for church school/youth leaders and worship team: There are many ways to make the well-known passages of Genesis fresh and dynamic. Following are several ideas that can be used separately, or mixed and matched.

1) "Speak Creation." This drama can be effectively used with readers alone. Choose a variety of voices—young and old, male and female—to portray God, and match them to the events of creation.

2) "Hear Creation." Prepare a tape of nature sounds to correspond to the reading. Allow about 10 seconds of sound time before or after each "day." (Day 1, 45 seconds of wind; Day 2, 45 seconds of rain storms; Day 3, 45 seconds of waves and light rain; Day 4, 1 minute of "light" sounds such as plucked violin strings or harp music; Day 5, 45 seconds of birds and whales; Day 6, 1 minute of birds and animals, plus 30 seconds of muted voices and laughter).

3) "Build Creation." Create a bulletin board display as the passage is read. Prepare pictures of needed elements in advance. This method is especially effective with children of all ages who will enjoy helping make the display.

4) "Watch Creation." Have one or two artists in the congregation paint creation on a large paper mural as the passage is read, using a simple, caricature style.

God's World

Genesis 1:1—2:4a
Easter Vigil, Years A B C

Key message: "In the beginning God...." Thus begins our Bible, as well as our understanding of God. God created a world of beauty and delight that is threatened by the chaos of evil. The same good God who gave us a good world, also gave us Jesus Christ, so that the world may be saved from evil and restored to what God intended. God's world, infused from the beginning with love and majesty, is forever made new by the death and resurrection of Jesus.

Cast: Narrator and 6 Voices of God.

VOICE 1 OF GOD: In the beginning, when I created the heavens and the earth, the earth was without life. Darkness covered the face of the deep, and my spirit swept over raging waters. Then I commanded, "Let there be light!" And I saw that the light was good. I separated the light from the darkness. The light would be called Day, and the darkness Night.

NARRATOR: And there was evening, and there was morning, the first day.

VOICE 2 OF GOD: "Let there be a dome in the midst of the waters!" I commanded. "Let it separate the waters above from the waters below."

NARRATOR: God made the dome and separated the waters that were under the dome from the waters above. God called the dome Sky. And there was evening and there was morning, the second day.

VOICE 3 OF GOD: Then I said, "Let the waters under the sky be gathered together into one place, and let dry land appear!" And it was so. I called the dry land Earth, and the waters that were gathered together I called Oceans. I commanded the earth to bring forth vegetation: plants, grains, and fruit trees of every kind. I looked at what I had done, and it was good.

NARRATOR: And there was evening and there was morning, the third day.

VOICE 4 OF GOD: Let there be lights in the sky to separate the day from the night! They will show the seasons and days and years. Let them shine down on the earth.

NARRATOR: And it was so. God made the two great lights—the sun to rule the day and the moon to rule the night—and the stars. God set them in the sky to give light to the earth.

VOICE 4 OF GOD: They shall rule over the day and over the night, and separate the light from the darkness.

NARRATOR: And so it was. God saw that it was good. And there was evening and there was morning, the fourth day.

VOICE 5 OF GOD: I ordered the oceans to bring forth a multitude of living creatures, and I let birds fly above the earth across the sky. I created the great sea monsters and fish of every kind, and every kind of bird. And it was good. I blessed them, saying, "Be fruitful and multiply. Fill the seas, and let birds cover the earth."

NARRATOR: And there was evening, and there was morning, the fifth day.

VOICE 6 OF GOD: "Let the earth bring forth living creatures of every kind," I proclaimed. "Tame animals, reptiles, and wild animals shall roam the earth!"

NARRATOR: And God created every type of animal, and every creature that creeps on the ground. And God saw that it was good.

VOICE 6 OF GOD: Let us make human beings in our image and likeness. They will have power over the fish of the sea, over the birds of the air, and over all the animals and reptiles of the earth.

NARRATOR: So humans were created in the image of God, both men and women. And God blessed them.

VOICE 6 OF GOD: Be fruitful and multiply; populate the earth. Take care of the fish in the seas, the birds in the air, and all living things that move upon the earth. I have given you every plant that yields grain, and every fruit tree for food. And to the beasts of the earth, the birds of the air, and to every other living creature, I have given green plants for food.

NARRATOR: And so it was. God saw everything that was made, and was very pleased. And there was evening and there was morning, the sixth day.

Thus the whole universe was completed. And on the seventh day, God was finished working and rested. So God blessed the seventh day and made it holy, because on that day God rested from all the work that had been done in creation. And that is how the world was created.

Deliverance

Exodus 14:10-31; 15:20-21
Easter Vigil, Years A B C

Before you begin...

The well-known eighth-century Easter hymn attributed to John of Damascus begins with references to the Exodus, instead of to the cross and empty tomb as we might expect.

> Come, you faithful, raise the strain of triumphant gladness!
> God has brought all Israel into joy from sadness,
> Loosed from Pharaoh's bitter yoke Jacob's sons and daughters,
> Led them with unmoistened foot through the Red Sea waters.
> (*Lutheran Book of Worship*, #132)

The church has long associated the death and resurrection of Jesus with the liberation of the Jews from slavery in Egypt and the annual celebration of Passover. The gospel accounts maintain that Good Friday and Easter coincided with that ancient festival. As God saved the Hebrews from oppression and led them to freedom, so Christ, by his passion, saves us from sin and evil, freeing us to serve God and God's people. The former slaves *passed over* from injustice to new life. Jesus, on this holy night, *passes over* from death to life and wins for us new life. In another hymn called "The Day of Resurrection," John of Damascus describes Easter as "the Passover of gladness, the Passover of God. From death to life eternal...our Christ brought us over..." (*Lutheran Book of Worship*, #141).

The Easter Vigil is also the time when baptismal candidates have traditionally been received into the church. The image of the Hebrews passing through the waters of the Red Sea on their passage to freedom is an analogy for what God does in baptism. God crushed the power of Pharaoh, drowning him and his army in the Red Sea so that the Israelites could be free. In the baptismal waters, our old, sinful selves "die" and we "rise" to freedom, following Jesus, who on this "night of nights," passes from death to life.

Through the Exodus, Israel learned that God is faithful, powerful, and willing to save. Christians similarly remember on this night that Christ is a mighty Savior who, through his dying and rising, delivers us from death and brings us to new life. Passing through the Red Sea waters, the Jews received their identity as God's people and were sealed to God forever. In the waters of baptism, we, too, are marked as children of the God to whom we eternally belong through Christ.

God made once-mighty Pharaoh helpless. Death, sin, injustice, and evil itself are now rendered ultimately powerless, because of what God has done through Jesus Christ. We can therefore live without fear and proclaim with our Hebrew ancestors: "Sing to the LORD, for [God] has triumphed gloriously" (Exod. 15:1).

Duration: 5–7 minutes.

Costumes: long white flowing gown for the Angel, gray cape for the Cloud (long enough for the bottom corners of the cape to be pinned to the wrist cuffs of the Cloud's shirt), rough-looking tunics/robes for Moses, Miriam, and all Israelites; short tunics and chest and back armor for Egyptians; blue tunics or extra fabric to camouflage stage assistants.

Props: walking stick, 2 sheets of blue fabric (8 feet long and 36–54 inches wide), shields and swords for Egyptian soldiers, tambourine, microphone.

Stage assistants: 4 to move the Red Sea.

Notes for church school/youth leaders and worship team: This is a short drama with a large cast and simple, but effective, special effects. It is especially exciting for children and young persons to perform, and is well suited to intergenerational worship. A large stage area of at least 20-feet by 10-feet is very helpful because so many people appear at once. If costumes are not available for everyone, have all of the Israelites dress in one color and the Egyptians in a contrasting color.

Deliverance

Exodus 14:10-31; 15:20-21

Easter Vigil, Years A B C

Key message: Through Moses, God delivered the Israelites from the Egyptians. This is our God: one who does not allow us to suffer forever, but ultimately rescues us from sin, separation, and oppression. What God did for the Israelites through Moses, God now does for us through Jesus' death and resurrection, bringing us through the water of baptism and establishing us on the dry ground of new life.

Cast: 7 speaking parts, (14–20 nonspeaking): Narrator, Israelite 1, Israelite 2, (2–6 more Israelites), Moses, Voice of God, (Angel), (Cloud), Egyptian, (4-6 Egyptian army), Miriam, (2 Israelite women)(4 stage assistants to portray the Red Sea).

(ANGEL of God and CLOUD enter stage left, followed by MOSES, MIRIAM, and ISRAELITES. Stop center stage. ISRAELITES appear frightened and keep looking behind them, whispering to each other.)

NARRATOR: Moses led the Israelite people out of slavery in Egypt. Pharaoh (FEHR-oh), the king of Egypt, was angry and tried to recapture them. As Pharaoh drew near, the Israelites looked back and saw the Egyptian army quickly advancing on them. In great fear they cried out to the Lord for help, and blamed Moses for their plight.

ISRAELITE 1: Wasn't there enough room in Egypt for our graves? Is that why you have taken us away to die in the wilderness?

ISRAELITE 2: What have you done to us, bringing us out of Egypt?

ISRAELITE 1: Didn't we tell you in Egypt to leave us alone and let us serve the Egyptians?

ISRAELITE 2: We would be better off serving the Egyptians than dying in the wilderness!

MOSES: Do not be afraid! Stand firm, and see how the Lord delivers us today. We will never see the Egyptians again. The Lord will save us. Keep still and watch!

(MOSES prays silently.)

VOICE OF GOD: *(not visible to listeners)* Moses, why do you cry out to me? Tell the Israelites to go forward. Raise your staff, and stretch out your hand over the sea. The water will divide in half and the Israelites will be able to walk through on dry ground. Then I will make the Egyptians so stubborn that they will follow them into the sea. I will show my power over Pharaoh and his entire army. And the Egyptians shall know that I am the Lord.

NARRATOR: The angel of God, who had been leading the Israelites, went behind them. A cloud, which had also been in front, moved between the Israelites and the army of Egypt. And so the cloud lit up the night for the Israelites, but kept the Egyptians in darkness. And the one did not come near the other all night.

(ANGEL of God and CLOUD move behind the Israelites. CLOUD holds out arms to shield the ISRAELITES from the EGYPTIANS. Enter STAGE ASSISTANTS stage right. Each holds one end of the two pieces of long blue fabric. They should stretch the fabric out at waist height, moving it to resemble waves.)

NARRATOR: Then Moses stretched out his hand over the sea. *(MOSES stretches out his walking stick.)* All night, the Lord drove the sea back by a strong east wind. The waters were divided and turned the sea into dry land.

(The two pairs of ASSISTANTS move apart, and hold the fabric like a wall to form a path in the water. The ISRAELITES pass through.)

NARRATOR: The Israelites walked into the sea on dry ground. The water formed a wall for them on their right and on their left. All of Pharaoh's soldiers, chariots, and horses went into the sea after them.

(EGYPTIANS enter the path between the waters. They pantomime loss of balance and panic. STAGE ASSISTANTS start waving the walls.)

NARRATOR: At dawn, God looked down upon the Egyptian army from a fiery cloud, and threw the Egyptians into panic. Their chariot wheels were clogged with mud, and they could hardly turn.

EGYPTIAN: Let us flee from the Israelites, for the Lord is fighting for them and against us.

VOICE OF GOD: Moses, stretch your hand over the sea, so that the water may come and drown the Egyptians and their chariots. *(MOSES stretches out his walking stick.)*

NARRATOR: So Moses stretched out his hand over the sea, and at dawn the sea returned to its normal depth. The Egyptians tried to flee, but the waters covered the chariots, soldiers, and horses.

(EGYPTIANS sink to the ground. STAGE ASSISTANTS return water to its original position, covering the EGYPTIANS.)

NARRATOR: The entire army of Pharaoh had followed the Israelites into the sea, and not one of them lived. But the Israelites had walked through the sea on dry ground, the waters forming a wall for them on their right and on their left.

Thus the Lord saved Israel that day from the Egyptians. Israel saw the great work that the Lord had done. The people stood in awe and believed in the Lord and Moses, God's servant.

Then the prophet Miriam took a tambourine in her hand and all the women went with her and danced with tambourines.

(MIRIAM and WOMEN dance.)

MIRIAM: Sing to the Lord, who has triumphed gloriously; horse and driver have been thrown into the sea!

ALL: Sing to the Lord, who has triumphed gloriously; horse and driver have been thrown into the sea!

(ALL exit joyfully.)

Who Is Jesus?

John: 20:1-18
Easter Day, Years A B C

Before you begin...

Again and again, the characters in John's gospel grapple with crucial questions concerning Jesus' identity and their relationship with him. A few people in this gospel immediately recognize Jesus as the Son of God and the Messiah. Others gradually come to understand his significance. And some never do.

Like many characters in John's gospel, when she first sees the risen Jesus, Mary Magdalene does not immediately recognize him or understand what the encounter means. Belief is seldom easy in John's gospel, even for those closest to Jesus.

Peter and the beloved disciple also struggle to understand the risen Lord. After Mary's discovery of the empty tomb and her initial report to them, they run to the garden and peer into the grave. Finding her story to be true and the body gone, they return home. John explains, "As yet they did not understand...that [Jesus] must rise from the dead" (John 20:9).

But Jesus reveals himself as the one whom God has sent, so that all will believe in him and have eternal life (3:16). He does not leave Mary in her grief and unfaith, but takes the initiative, calling her by name. Mary immediately recognizes Jesus and has no doubt about her relationship with him. She responds to him with a deeply personal term, "Rabbouni" (My dear Rabbi), signifying the intimate nature of her relationship with him. Jesus instructs her to go and tell the good news to the other disciples. Thus, Mary becomes the first witness to the risen Christ.

With his death on the cross and subsequent resurrection, Jesus brings all people to God through himself. "When I am lifted up from the earth, I will draw all people to myself" (12:32). Jesus' victory over death on Easter is, at least for Mary, a convincing answer to those perennial questions of faith: Who is Jesus? and Who is he to me?

Duration: 3 minutes.

Costumes: white robes for Jesus and angels, simple tunics or robes for Peter and disciples, plain robe and headdress for Mary Magdalene.

Props: tomb and large rock (See "Notes for church school/youth leaders and worship team"), bundle of white cloth strips, folded white cloth, wooden table, benches or several chairs, spotlight.

Optional props: dishes and food for the table.

Stage assistant: 1 person to work spotlight.

Notes for church school/youth leaders and worship team: The last 4 dramas in this book, Easter Day through Pentecost Day, can be grouped together to form a 4-act play lasting about 12 minutes. The house in which the disciples hide is common to all 4 readings. Other locations are the tomb, the road and inn at Emmaus, and the area outside the disciples' hideout.

For this reading, you will need a tomb large enough to hold several people. Two portable chalk/bulletin boards or screens spaced about 4 feet apart and draped with heavy gray or tan cloth will work well. The large rock can be simulated with cardboard or plywood, or made out of papier-mâché. You will probably need a spotlight directed at the interior of the tomb, so viewers can clearly see the action. The angels should be able to enter and exit through the back of the tomb.

The disciples' house can be as simple as a wooden table with benches or chairs around it. Most of the action in the drama is pantomimed; so more complex props are not essential. The tomb and house should be at opposite ends of the stage area—the tomb stage left, and the house stage right.

Who Is Jesus?

John: 20:1-18

Easter Day, Years A B C

Key message: The victory that Jesus has already won on the cross is extended with his resurrection. By raising Jesus from the dead, God confirms that Jesus is the one who reconciles us to God and gives abundant life. As Jesus offers his grace to Mary in her disbelief and sorrow, so Jesus appears to us today, giving us eternal life with God. Therefore, we testify with Mary: we have not seen a mere gardener; we have seen the Lord—our Lord.

Cast: 4 speaking, (5 or more nonspeaking): Narrator, Mary Magdalene, (Peter), (Beloved disciple), (2 or more Disciples), Angel 1, (Angel 2), Jesus.

(PETER, BELOVED DISCIPLE, and OTHER DISCIPLES are sitting around the table looking frightened and depressed. MARY MAGDALENE enters stage right and walks toward the tomb.)

NARRATOR: Early on Sunday morning, while it was still dark, Mary Magdalene went to the tomb and saw that the stone in front of the entrance had been removed.

([Spotlight on, focused inside tomb.] MARY looks in tomb, gasps, and runs to the disciples' hideout.)

NARRATOR: She ran to find Simon Peter and the other disciple whom Jesus loved.

MARY MAGDALENE: *(breathless and agitated)* Peter, Peter! They have taken the Lord from the tomb. I don't know where they have put him.

(PETER and BELOVED DISCIPLE pantomime the following action as the NARRATOR speaks. MARY follows them back to the tomb, and waits near the entrance, crying.)

NARRATOR: Peter and the other disciple set out toward the tomb. They were running together, but the other disciple outran Peter and reached the tomb first. He bent down, looked into the tomb, and saw the linen wrappings lying there, but he didn't go in. Simon Peter arrived and went inside the tomb. He, too, saw the linen wrappings lying there, but the cloth that had been on Jesus' head was rolled up in a place by itself. Then the other disciple also went in, and he saw and believed what Mary had said. *(PETER and DISCIPLE are very upset.)* At that time the disciples did not understand the scripture, which said that Jesus must rise from the dead. So Peter and the other disciple returned home.

([Spotlight off.] PETER and BELOVED DISCIPLE sadly return to room. In pantomime they explain to the others what they found. ANGELS quietly enter the tomb from the back.)

NARRATOR: But Mary stood weeping outside the tomb. *[Spotlight on.]* As she wept, she looked into the tomb, and saw two angels in white. They were sitting where Jesus' body had been, one by the head and the other at the feet.

ANGEL 1: Woman, why are you weeping?

MARY MAGDALENE: They have taken away my Lord, and I do not know where they have put him.

(Enter JESUS stage left.)

NARRATOR: After Mary said this, she turned around and saw Jesus standing there, but she did not know that it was Jesus. She thought he was the gardener.

JESUS: Woman, why are you crying? Who are you looking for?

MARY MAGDALENE: Sir, if you have moved my Lord's body, tell me where you have put him, and I will take him away. *(She turns away. [Spotlight on JESUS])*

JESUS: *(softly)* Mary!

MARY MAGDALENE: Rabbouni! (rah-BOON-ee) My dear Teacher! *(She goes toward JESUS with her arms outstretched.)*

JESUS: Don't hold on to me! I have not yet ascended to heaven. But go to my disciples and say to them, "I am ascending to my Father and your Father, to my God and your God."

(MARY reluctantly leaves JESUS and goes back to the DISCIPLES. JESUS exits. ANGELS exit through back of tomb.)

NARRATOR: Mary Magdalene went back to the disciples—

MARY MAGDALENE: I have seen the Lord!

NARRATOR:—and she told them everything that he had said to her. *(MARY pantomimes conversation to the DISCIPLES.)*

To Believe and to Share

John: 20:19-31

Easter 2, Years A B C

Before you begin...

In John 20:19-23, Jesus appears to the disciples for the first time since his cruci-fixion. His appearance confirms what Mary has told them: he is alive, not dead. To prove his identity, Jesus shows them his wounded hands and side. He hopes that they will have faith and believe—not only that he is alive, but that he is the one sent by God to conquer the world (16:33), and that he will soon return to that same God (20:17).

Thomas is not with the group when Jesus first appears to them. The others tell him the same good news that Mary told them in verse 18: "We have seen the Lord" (20:25). Thomas replies, "Unless I see the mark of the nails in his hands, and put my finger in the mark of the nails and my hand in his side, I will not believe" (20:25).

Thomas is indeed a doubter. It is not fair, however, to conclude from his famous comment that he doubts more than the other disciples do. After all, what Thomas wants is no more than the evidence that Jesus has already given the others (20:20).

Thomas gets what he wants. Jesus invites his friend to inspect and touch—and convinces Thomas of the fundamental truth: Jesus, who once was dead, is now alive. This scripture passage is not only about Thomas's doubt; it is about Jesus' actions to bring Thomas and the other disciples to faith. Jesus' mission is to do whatever is necessary, including dying on a cross, so that, like Thomas, all may proclaim: "My Lord and my God!" (20:28).

In this passage, Jesus also commissions the disciples: "As the Father has sent me, so I send you" (20:21). He breathes on them, giving the Holy Spirit, and then con-fers the authority to forgive sins. Jesus gives his followers the responsibility—and the power—to serve the world as he did, so that his ministry will continue after he ascends. Because of the similarity of these events to those recorded in Acts 1 and 2, this passage is often called "John's Pentecost."

In the concluding verses, we are invited to believe in Jesus' resurrection, even though we cannot see or touch his body. In verse 31, John sums up the purpose of the gospel: that we "may come to believe that Jesus is the Messiah, the Son of God, and through believing...have life in his name." Jesus wants us to believe in him—not because we have seen him physically, but because he gives new life. He also wants us to continue his ministry of bringing people to God.

Duration: 2–3 minutes.

Costumes: white robe for Jesus, simple tunics or robes for the disciples.

Props: wooden table, benches or several chairs, screen or curtain, spotlight.

Optional props: dishes and food for the table.

Stage assistant: 1 person to work spotlight.

Notes for church school/youth leaders and worship team: The setting and action in this reading are simple. How Jesus enters and exits, however, can significantly affect the dramatic impact. Jesus needs to be waiting close to the disciples, yet concealed from view. One solution is a folding screen positioned toward the back of the stage around which Jesus can quietly emerge. A curtain is another option.

To Believe and to Share

John: 20:19-31

Easter 2, Years A B C

Key message: Jesus has one goal for the disciples, Thomas, and the world: that all would believe in him and thereby live with God forever. This is his mission, and, through the gift of the Holy Spirit, is ours as well: to tell and live the story of Jesus so that all may know him and the God who sent him.

Cast: 4 speaking, (5–10 nonspeaking): Narrator, Jesus, Disciple 1, Thomas, (5–10 Disciples).

(DISCIPLE 1 and DISCIPLES sit and stand around the table talking quietly. JESUS stands behind the screen, and quietly enters as NARRATOR speaks.)

NARRATOR: Late Sunday evening, the disciples met behind locked doors because they were afraid of the religious authorities. Suddenly, Jesus stood among them.

[Spotlight on JESUS.]

JESUS: Peace be with you!

NARRATOR: After saying this, he showed them his hands and his side. *(JESUS walks toward the DISCIPLES and shows them his hands.)* The disciples rejoiced when they saw the Lord.

JESUS: Peace be with you. As the Father has sent me, so I send you. *(breathes on the DISCIPLES)* Receive the Holy Spirit. If you forgive anyone's sins, they are forgiven; if you do not forgive their sins, they shall remain.

(JESUS walks toward back of stage. [Spotlight off.] JESUS goes behind the screen.)

NARRATOR: But Thomas, one of the twelve called the twin, was not with them when Jesus came.

(Enter THOMAS.)

DISCIPLE 1: Thomas! We have seen the Lord! *(All DISCIPLES nod excitedly.)*

THOMAS: Unless I see the marks of the nails in his hands, and put my finger on the marks and my hand in his side, I will not believe.

(JESUS quietly enters as NARRATOR speaks.)

NARRATOR: A week later the disciples were again gathered in the house and Thomas was with them. Although the doors were shut, Jesus came and stood among them.

[Spotlight on JESUS.]

JESUS: Peace be with you! *(to THOMAS)* Put your finger here and see my hands. Reach out your hand and put it in my side. Do not doubt but believe!

THOMAS: *(falls to his knees)* My Lord and my God!

JESUS: Have you believed because you have seen me? Happy are those who have not seen and yet have come to believe.

(JESUS talks to DISCIPLES as NARRATOR speaks.)

NARRATOR: Now Jesus did many other miracles in the presence of his disciples, which are not written down. But these are written so that you may believe that Jesus is the Messiah, the Son of God. Through your faith you will have life in Jesus' name.

We Meet Him in Church

Luke 24:13-35
Easter 3, Year A; Easter Evening, A B C

Before you begin...

It is important to remember that the gospels were written many years after Jesus' death and resurrection. Like the other gospel writers, Luke wrote his story for a Christian community that had already existed for several decades. Although he drew upon sources that extended back to the ministry of Jesus, he selected and shaped that material to address a church that had no firsthand knowledge of Jesus. Luke's community no doubt had questions much like those we Christians have today: "How can we, who were not alive when Jesus walked the earth, experience him?" To answer that question, Luke included the story commonly called "The Road to Emmaus."

It is a wonderfully told and much beloved story. Two disciples are returning home following the events that transpired in Jerusalem during Passover. They are understandably sad because Jesus, whom they "had hoped [to be] the one to redeem Israel" (Luke 24:21), has been executed. They are puzzled, however, by reports from other disciples who claim that angels have told them Jesus is alive, not dead (24:23).

As the account unfolds, we sense that Cleopas and his friend, not unlike members of Luke's church and ours today, are aching for the presence of Jesus. The irony, of course, is that Jesus, whom they so deeply desire, is walking with them on the road, "but their eyes [are] kept from recognizing him" (24:16).

Jesus is not content to remain hidden and reveals himself to the disciples in two ways. First, their hearts "burn" within them (24:32) as he explains scripture to them. Rather than speaking about the Bible in a general way, he interprets scripture so that the truth "about himself" (24:27) is revealed—that is, so that he himself is made known. Likewise, Jesus discloses his presence when he takes bread, blesses, breaks, and gives it to them (24:30).

Because Luke's readers constituted a church, they undoubtedly worshiped every week through the hearing of scripture and the celebration of communion. Therefore, they must have heard in this story a summary of their own Sunday worship, a liturgy of word and sacrament. The living Jesus, sometimes so difficult to perceive, is revealed when the church gathers on the Lord's day to hear the word and feast at his table.

This is good news for the church today, as well: Jesus wants to make himself known to us. He is not far away. Indeed, we meet him at church!

Duration: 2–3 minutes.

Costumes: simple tunics or robes for all.

Props: 2 wooden tables, chairs or benches, food for the table at the inn—including a small loaf of bread and a wine cup, folding screen.

Optional prop: spotlight.

Stage assistant: 1 person to work spotlight.

Notes for church school/youth leaders and worship team: The conversations taking place in this drama are full of conflicting emotions—sadness, confusion, amazement, and excitement—that convey the feelings of the disciples on Easter day. Once again, Jesus disappears after revealing himself to his disciples, this time in the inn at Emmaus. To capture the impact of this amazing experience, you will need to position a folding screen or curtain near the inn table so Jesus can quickly exit. Shine the spotlight on Jesus at the moment when Cleopas and the disciple recognize him.

NOTE: When Jesus reenacts the Last Supper, it is very important theologically that there be four specific acts relative to the bread: taking, blessing, breaking, and giving. Breaking the bread requires making a slight cut in the bottom of the loaf. For dramatic and historic purposes, a whole loaf is better than a partial loaf or a piece of sliced bread. A whole piece of pita bread will work well. A common Jewish blessing has been added to the reading for Jesus to say over the bread.

We Meet Him in Church

Luke 24:13-35

Easter 3, Year A; Easter Evening, A B C

Key message: Frightened and sad, Cleopas and the other disciple do not immediately recognize Jesus. As Jesus explains the words in the Bible and breaks bread with them, however, they know that it is he and see that he is indeed alive. We, too, can experience the risen Jesus by hearing and understanding the scriptures, and by sharing the bread and the cup with the community of Jesus' followers: the church.

Cast: 5 speaking, (4–8 nonspeaking): Narrator, Jesus, Cleopas, Disciple 1, Disciple 2, (4–8 Disciples).

(Stage should be set with one table and chairs in the stage right background for the disciples' house, and the other table and chairs in the stage left foreground for the inn. CLEOPAS and DISCIPLE 1 are walking from the disciples' house toward the inn. They are deep in conversation. JESUS enters and joins them.)

NARRATOR: On the same Sunday after Jesus died, two of his disciples were walking to a village called Emmaus (eh-MAY-uhs), about seven miles from Jerusalem. As they walked and discussed all the things that had happened, Jesus himself came near and started walking with them. But they didn't recognize him.

JESUS: What are you talking about as you walk along?

(CLEOPAS and DISCIPLE 1 stop and turn to JESUS. They shake their heads sadly.)

CLEOPAS: Are you the only visitor in Jerusalem who doesn't know about the things that have taken place these last few days?

JESUS: What things?

CLEOPAS: The things about Jesus of Nazareth, who was a powerful prophet in words and actions before God and all the people.

DISCIPLE 1: Our chief priests and leaders handed him over to be condemned to death and crucified!

CLEOPAS: *(sadly)* We had hoped that he would be the one to free Israel.

DISCIPLE 1: Yes. It has now been three days since these things took place. Then today, some women of our group surprised us. They went to the tomb early this morning, but Jesus' body wasn't there. They told us that they had seen a vision of angels who said that Jesus was alive!

CLEOPAS: Others in our group went to the tomb and found it just as the women had said; but they didn't see Jesus either.

JESUS: Oh, how foolish you are, and how slow of heart to believe all that the prophets have said! Didn't you know that the Messiah had to suffer these things and then enter his glory?

(JESUS, CLEOPAS, and DISCIPLE 1 begin walking again while JESUS speaks.)

NARRATOR: Then beginning with Moses and all the prophets, he explained to them the things written about himself in the scriptures. When they came to the village where the disciples planned to stop for the night, Jesus kept walking as if continuing on.

DISCIPLE 1: *(insistently)* Sir, stay with us. It is almost evening, and it will be dark soon.

(CLEOPAS, DISCIPLE 1, and JESUS go into the inn and sit at the table. [Spotlight on JESUS.])

NARRATOR: So Jesus went in with them. When he was at the table, he took bread, blessed and broke it, and gave it to them.

(JESUS stands. He distinctly lifts up the bread, blesses it, breaks it, and gives it to the disciples.)

JESUS: *(lifting the bread)* Blessed are you, O Lord our God, ruler of the universe, who feeds the entire world in your goodness, with grace, loving kindness, and compassion. You give bread to all flesh, for your mercy is forever.

(JESUS breaks the bread and gives pieces to CLEOPAS and DISCIPLE 1 who eat it. As they bow their heads in prayer, JESUS slips behind screen. [Spotlight off.] CLEOPAS and DISCIPLE 1 look at each other in astonishment.)

NARRATOR: Then their eyes were opened, and they recognized him; and he vanished from their sight.

DISCIPLE 1: Didn't you feel your heart burning within you when he talked to us on the road?

CLEOPAS: Yes, yes! While he was explaining the scriptures to us!

NARRATOR: They got up at once and returned to Jerusalem. They found Jesus' disciples and companions gathered together.

(CLEOPAS and DISCIPLE 1 hurry back to disciples' house. As they enter DISCIPLE 2 runs up to them.)

DISCIPLE 2: The Lord has risen! He appeared to Simon!

(ALL start talking excitedly.)

NARRATOR: Then the two disciples told the others what had happened to them on the road, and how Jesus had made himself known in the breaking of bread.

Everyone…Shall Be Saved

Acts 2:1-21
Pentecost, Years A B C

Before you begin…

In the North American context, Pentecost Day comes at the end of the nine-month school year, prior to the start of summer when some types of activities slow down considerably. For North Americans, then, Pentecost signals the beginning of a time of rest—and perhaps even disengagement from the community of faith. How ironic! In the book of Acts, Pentecost was the beginning of the church, not the end.

Pentecost is the Greek name for an ancient Jewish festival known as the Feast of Weeks—a celebration concluding seven weeks of harvest that began at Passover. At the feast, the people gave thanks to God for the harvest. Leviticus 23:15-21 dictates the proper way to observe the Feast of Weeks: "You shall hold a holy convocation" (Lev. 23:21).

Thousands of Jews were celebrating the Feast of Weeks in Jerusalem when the strange events described in Acts 2 took place. The prevailing mood of the Feast of Weeks, that of joy and thanksgiving for the abundant and life-giving blessings of God, must have inspired Jesus' disciples. Luke reports, "All of them were filled with the Holy Spirit" (Acts 2:4).

The apostles, as Jewish people, were acquainted with the notion of God's Spirit as a living and powerful reality in the lives of the faithful. Also, they had experienced the Spirit in the person and ministry of Jesus. For the last fifty days they had witnessed the wonder of the risen Christ. And Jesus had promised the gift of the Holy Spirit to the disciples if they waited for it in Jerusalem (1:4-5). The disciples were engaged in earnest and hopeful prayer as they waited for the gift that Jesus had promised (1:14).

The Pentecost event described in this scripture passage is remarkable in two ways. The first notable aspect is the dramatic way in which the Holy Spirit descends upon and possesses the apostles: "a violent wind" and "tongues…of fire" enable them to speak in other languages (2:2-4). None of the disciples could have predicted the way in which God's Spirit would come to them. The second remarkable part of Pentecost is that the gift of the Spirit is not for the disciples alone, but for the entire world. People of various nationalities hear the good news proclaimed (2:5-11).

The result of Pentecost, too, is unexpected. Instantly, this band of inwardly oriented followers becomes a group of international evangelists. For example, Peter, who before only addressed fellow believers (1:15-22), becomes a missionary to the nations (2:14-36).

And what did Peter and the others proclaim? "…God's deeds of power" (2:11). Indeed, this is what Pentecost, and its predecessor, the Feast of Weeks, celebrate: that God is a mighty Spirit of goodness and love. Filled with that Spirit, the church today can abide no period of hibernation, but is compelled to repeat Peter's message: "...everyone who calls on the name of the Lord shall be saved" (2:21).

Duration: 5 minutes.

Costumes: simple tunics or robes for the disciples and people in crowd, head coverings for the women.

Props: wooden table, benches or several chairs, floor or table fan, overhead projector, prepared transparency (See "Notes for church school/youth leaders and worship team").

Optional prop: audiotape of strong wind.

Stage assistants: 1 to work overhead, 1 to operate the fan.

Notes for church school/youth leaders and worship team: The effect of the Holy Spirit descending on the disciples can be powerfully portrayed with a few easy props. A hidden fan and an audiotape of the sound of wind can simulate the "violent wind." To make the tongues of fire, use a piece of black construction paper large enough to cover the entire lighted surface of the overhead projector. Cut about 12 flame-shaped holes in the paper. Cover the holes with overlapping red and yellow cellophane and tape down the edges. Position the black paper on the overhead so that when the overhead light is turned on, only the flames will be projected on the wall.

After the disciples have been filled with the Holy Spirit, they begin to speak in foreign languages. The actors portraying the disciples have been given foreign phrases to shout out. Depending on the ethnic makeup of your church, you may want to substitute different languages.

Pronunciation guide (also included on page 6):

syllable:	as in:
ah	water
a	cat
eh	net
ee	feet
oh	boat
oo	boot
aw	awe
uh	dull
ih	sit
ay	day
rr	flipped "r"
ch	soft "ch" sound, like "Bach"

Everyone...Shall Be Saved

Acts 2:1-21

Pentecost, Years A B C

Key message: God's Spirit descended upon the disciples, driving them into the city streets to announce to all the good news of Jesus. The outpouring of the Holy Spirit started with the Twelve, but quickly moved to the masses. Therefore, God's mission is no less than the salvation of all humanity. As the Spirit empowered the disciples to participate in that mission long ago, so we are empowered today.

Cast: 8 speaking, (2–8 nonspeaking): Narrator, Peter, Disciple 1, Disciple 2, Disciple 3, Crowd 1, Crowd 2, Crowd 3, (2–8 extras in the crowd).

(The DISCIPLES are gathered around the table talking quietly.)

NARRATOR: When the day of Pentecost had come, all of Jesus' disciples were gathered together in one place. *[Start fan and tape of the wind.]* Suddenly from heaven there came the sound of a violent wind, and it filled the entire house where they were meeting. *(pause) [Turn on overhead projector.]* Then, what looked like tongues of fire appeared among them, and a flame rested on each one. They were filled with the Holy Spirit and were given the ability to speak in other languages. *[Turn off fan and tape.]*

(PETER, DISCIPLE 1, DISCIPLE 2, and DISCIPLE 3 should shout out their lines simultaneously several times, getting progressively louder. They leave the house and stand in the street. [Turn off overhead projector.])

PETER: Benedicat vos omnipotens Deus! (beh-neh-DEE-caht vohs ohm-NEE-poh-tehns DEH-oos) (Latin: May almighty God bless you!)

DISCIPLE 1: ¡Cristo nuestro Salvador ha resucitado! (KRREES-toh noo-EH-strroh SAHL-vah-dohrr ah rreh-soo-see-TAH-doh) (Spanish: Christ our savior has risen!)

DISCIPLE 2: Iesusama wa wareware no shin no Meshia dearu! (ee-ay-soo-sah-mah wah wah-reh-wah-reh noh sheen noh meh-shee-ah day-ah-roo) (Japanese: Jesus is truly the Messiah!)

DISCIPLE 3: Christ notre Sauveur s'est revelé! (krreest NAW-trruh saw-VUHRR seh rreh-vehl-EH) (French: Christ our Savior has risen!)

PETER: Mwari Ngaakudzwe! (MWAH-ree NGAH-ah-KOO-dzway) (Shona from Zimbabwe: God be praised!)

DISCIPLE 1: Whidehashin Hananim gge Chanyang hara! (wee-deh-hahsh-een hahn-ahn-eem ghay chahn-yahng hah-rrah) (Korean: Praise our great God!)

DISCIPLE 2: Der Herr ist mächtig! (dehrr hehrr eest MEHCH-teech) (German: The Lord is mighty!)

DISCIPLE 3: Kyrie eléison! (KEE-rree-eh eh-LEH-ee-sawn) (Greek: Lord have mercy!)

(CROWD enters stage left and gathers around the disciples. They speak excitedly to each other. DISCIPLES speak more quietly.)

NARRATOR: Now there were devout Jews from every nation under heaven living in Jerusalem. As the sound of the disciples speaking grew louder, they gathered around them and were confused. Each heard his or her own native language. They spoke to one another in amazement.

CROWD 1: Aren't all these people who are speaking Galileans (gal-ih-LEE-ans)? How can we each be hearing our own native language?

CROWD 2: We come from Parthia (PAHR-thee-ah), Media (MEH-dee-ah), Elam (EE-lahm), and Mesopotamia (mehs-oh-poh-TAY-mee-ah), as well as Judea (joo-DEE-ah), Asia, Egypt and the parts of Libya!

CROWD 3: We are visitors from Rome, Crete, and Arabia. Some of us were born Jews—

CROWD 2:—and some of us have chosen to be Jews. But we all hear them speaking about God's wonderful deeds in our own languages!

CROWD 1: What does this mean?

CROWD 3: *(sneer)* They're drunk on new wine!

(CROWD starts to turn and walk away.)

NARRATOR: But Peter, who was standing with the other disciples, raised his voice and answered them.

(DISCIPLES stop speaking.)

PETER: People of Judea and all who live in Jerusalem, listen—and understand what I say. These people aren't drunk, as you suppose. It's only nine o'clock in the morning! No, this is what God spoke through the prophet Joel.

(CROWD stops and listens to PETER, but stays at a distance.)

PETER: *(in a clear, confident voice)* In the last days, God declares, I will pour out my Spirit upon everyone. Your sons and your daughters shall prophesy. Your young people shall see visions, and your old people shall dream dreams. Even upon my servants I will pour out my Spirit, and they shall prophesy.

(CROWD gathers around PETER. They become increasingly excited as he speaks.)

PETER: *(very dramatically, using arm gestures to act out the passage)* And I will work miracles in the heavens above and wondrous deeds on the earth below. There will be blood, and fire, and smoky mist. The sun shall turn dark and the moon will be the color of blood before the coming of the Lord's great and glorious day. Then everyone who cries to the Lord for help shall be saved.

(ALL exit into the congregation joyously proclaiming the glory of God. You may choose to end with the congregation singing a hymn as the actors exit.)